GROOVY
VIBES
Coloring Book
Iris Azalea

THIS BOOK BELONGS TO

COLORING TIPS

Thank you for purchasing this colouring book. Inside you will find 50 Inspirational Flower Power Hippies for you to relax, color and explore your creativity.

Each page has a blank side for potential bleed through with wet pens.

If you are using wet pens, please insert a blank page behind the page you are working on to prevent bleed through to the next coloring page.

You can test you colors on the Test pages in the front and back of this book.

I hope you enjoy this coloring book and would appreciate a review to help me as an independent publisher.

Happy Coloring

Iris Azalea

Color Test Page

Color Test Page

Other books you will enjoy by Iris Azalea

(Just type in the ASIN number in the Amazon Search bar or look through my Author page)

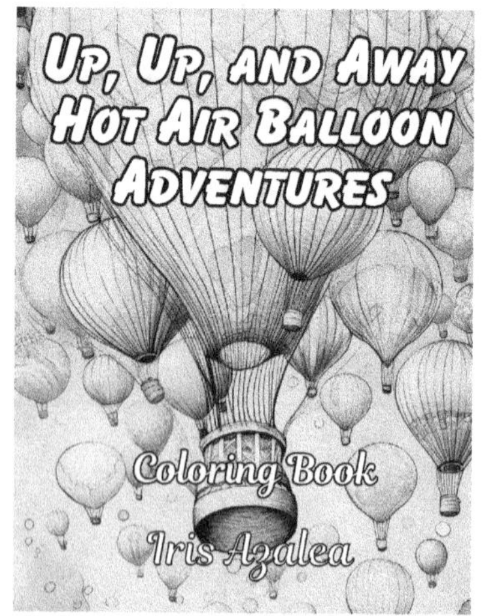

ASIN: B0C91X9ZSW

ASIN: B0C91MY794

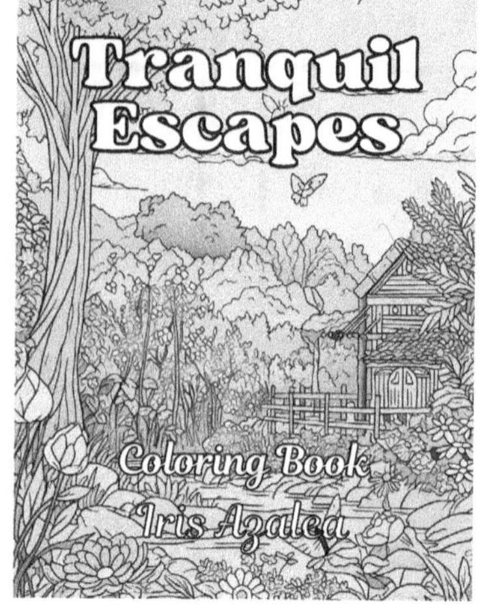

ASIN: B0C91DKFVL

ASIN: B0CCCVMX2H

ASIN: B0C91ZWN8N

ASIN: B0CCCQSJCB

ASIN: B0CCCPJHX9

ASIN: B0CCCPFF82

ASIN: B0C91MY79C